4 S's for Noticing Nature

by Heidi Ferris

Other Growing Green Hearts books in this series:

- 1-2-3 Earth, Air & Me
- 4 S's for Noticing Nature: Senses, Sun, Systems, Seasons
- 5 R's for Environment: Rethink, Reduce, Reuse, Recycle, Rejoice*
- 6 C's for Creation Care: Creation, Christ, Creativity, Combustion, Climate, Connect*
- 7 Water Wonderings
- 8 Butterfly Questions for Gardening

* Books that include science and faith together.

www.growinggreenhearts.com

Growing
Green Hearts®

About This Series

This series of books, Playing with Science and Systems, has been created to be simple, scientifically accurate, and sometimes focused on faith. Science is problem finding and problem solving. The author Heidi Ferris is passionate about encouraging youth to ask questions, boosting science literacy, empowering kids to care for our shared resources, and exploring the wonders in God's creation. Heidi lives in Minnesota with her family - not far from the Mississippi River.

—

This book is dedicated to future generations and those working to preserve and protect natural spaces and our shared resources.

Contents

 **4 S's for Noticing Nature**

4

Words that start with S:
1. Senses
2. Seasons
3. Sun
4. Systems

Our senses gather information about our world.
See, smell, hear, taste, touch. These are your senses.

7

When we notice something with our senses it is an observation. We can notice and observe things in nature. Scientists of all ages use observations to ask questions.

1 Senses

Just ask:

How does it work? Why does it smell good?
What does it sound like? Will it taste spicy?
Where will it feel smooth?

2 Seasons

The season depends upon the amount of sunlight each day. Every day is 24 hours long, but in some seasons the days have more or less sunlight.

Just ask:
What do you notice when the seasons change?

 Sun

Stars send energy into space. Energy comes to earth from the sun. Our sun is a star. It is the closest star to earth.

Planet earth is tilted to the side, not straight up and down.
This is why some places on earth have 4 seasons year round.

Where we live, earth tilted to the sun makes warm, long days of summer.

Where we live, earth tilted away from the sun makes chilly, dark days of winter. Plants and animals notice the changes too.

Plants notice light energy. Plant leaves collect light from the sun and turn it into food for the plant to grow.

4 System

A system is smaller parts working together.
Earth has four main systems: water, air, land, and living
things. Earth's systems and parts all work together.

Animals and plants can use air, water, soil and sunshine in different ways. These parts work together in systems.

Your body system gets food from plants or animals so you can move and play.

The amount of sunlight is the reason there are four seasons. Noticing changes is something you can do. When we use our senses to observe nature we find—

Nature is systems with parts intertwined!

Just ask:
How can you use your senses to notice nature?

Glossary

Senses: See, taste, smell, touch, hear to notice and learn about your world

Seasons: Parts of the year (winter, spring, summer, fall) marked by changes in weather and hours of daylight

Sun: Closest star to earth

System: Smaller parts working together

Observation: Noticing something using your senses

41275035R00017

Made in the USA
Middletown, DE
08 March 2017